A LOOK AT EARTH'S ROCKS

WHAT ARE METAMORPHIC ROCKS?

BY KRISTEN RAJCZAK NELSON

Gareth Stevens
PUBLISHING

CRASHCOURSE

Please visit our website, www.garethstevens.com. For a free color catalog of all our high-quality books, call toll free 1-800-542-2595 or fax 1-877-542-2596.

Library of Congress Cataloging-in-Publication Data

Names: Rajczak Nelson, Kristen.
Title: What are metamorphic rocks? / Kristen Rajczak Nelson.
Description: New York : Gareth Stevens Publishing, 2017. | Series: A look at earth's rocks | Includes index.
Identifiers: LCCN 2016031621| ISBN 9781482462487 (pbk. book) | ISBN 9781482462500 (6 pack) | ISBN 9781482462494 (library bound book)
Subjects: LCSH: Metamorphic rocks--Juvenile literature. | Petrology--Juvenile literature.
Classification: LCC QE475 .R285 2017 | DDC 552/.4--dc23
LC record available at https://lccn.loc.gov/2016031621

First Edition

Published in 2018 by
Gareth Stevens Publishing
111 East 14th Street, Suite 349
New York, NY 10003

Copyright © 2018 Gareth Stevens Publishing

Designer: Samantha DeMartin
Editor: Kristen Nelson

Photo credits: Series background winnond/Shutterstock.com; caption box Edhar Shvets/Shutterstock.com; cover, p. 1 Natalya Rozhkova/Shutterstock.com; pp. 5 (sedimentary), 15 (granite) Aerodim/Shutterstock.com; p. 5 (igneous) ShurikAK/Shutterstock.com; p. 5 (metamorphic) KPG_Payless/Shutterstock.com; p. 7 (limestone) Jariya_M/Shutterstock.com; p. 7 (marble) NeroRosso/Shutterstock.com; p. 9 Jason Edwards/National Geographic/Getty Images; p. 12 vvoe/Shutterstock.com; p. 13 (main) Nickola_Che/Shutterstock.com; p. 15 (gneiss) ChWeiss/Shutterstock.com; p. 17 Ammit Jack/Shutterstock.com; p. 19 DEA/D'ARCO EDITORI/De Agostini/Getty Images; p. 21 RICHARD BOUHET/AFP/Getty Images; p. 23 Nikitin Victor/Shutterstock.com; p. 25 Brazil Photos/Lightrocket/Getty Images; p. 27 (slate) Bunphot Kliaphuangphit/Shutterstock.com; p. 27 (phyllite) veou/Shutterstock.com; p. 29 David R. Tribble/Wikimedia Commons; p. 30 Doug Lemke/Shutterstock.com.

All rights reserved. No part of this book may be reproduced in any form without permission in writing from the publisher, except by a reviewer.

Printed in the United States of America

CPSIA compliance information: Batch #CS17GS: For further information contact Gareth Stevens, New York, New York at 1-800-542-2595.

CONTENTS

From Rock	4
Composition	6
Changing Conditions	10
Where's the Rock?	16
Kinds of Metamorphism	18
Texture	22
Schist	28
How Does Metamorphic Rock Form?	30
Glossary	31
For More Information	32
Index	32

Words in the glossary appear in **bold** type the first time they are used in the text.

FROM ROCK

There are three kinds of rocks: **sedimentary**, **igneous**, and metamorphic. Both sedimentary and igneous **processes** can create new rock. Metamorphic rock only forms from existing rock. However, it can form from any kind of rock—even other metamorphic rock!

SEDIMENTARY

IGNEOUS

METAMORPHIC

MAKE THE GRADE

The word "metamorphic" comes from the Greek words *meta*, which means "change," and *morphe*, which means "form." So "metamorphic" means "changing form."

COMPOSITION

Metamorphism is the changing of a rock's **chemical** or **physical** composition, or makeup. Metamorphism happens because of new conditions around the rock. The rock's composition changes in order to remain **stable** in the new conditions.

LIMESTONE
SEDIMENTARY ROCK

▶

MARBLE
METAMORPHIC ROCK

MAKE THE GRADE

Minerals are the matter in the ground that forms rocks.

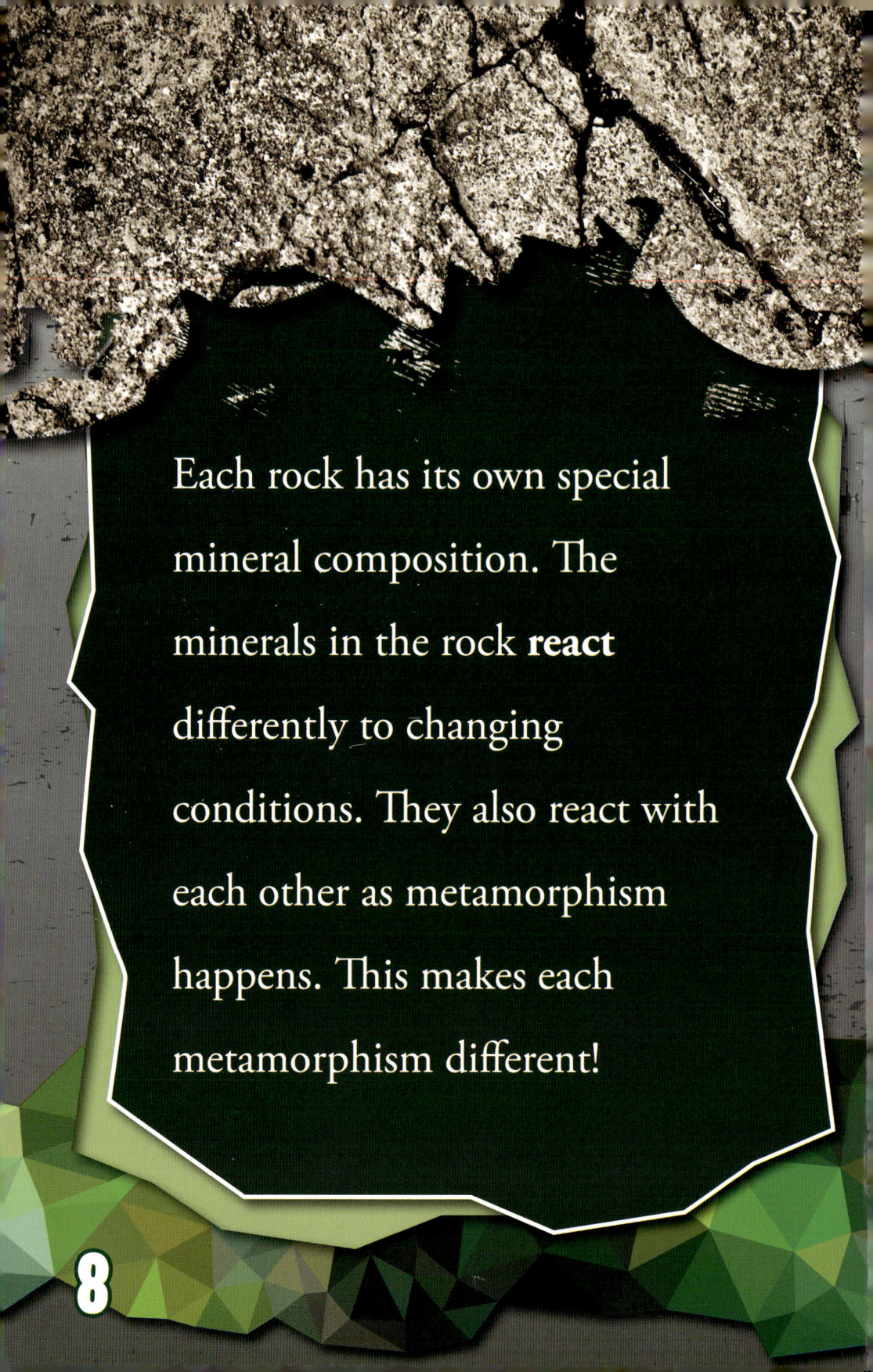

Each rock has its own special mineral composition. The minerals in the rock **react** differently to changing conditions. They also react with each other as metamorphism happens. This makes each metamorphism different!

MAKE THE GRADE

Many times, minerals change into different forms of themselves during metamorphism.

QUARTZ

CHANGING CONDITIONS

Heat and pressure are two conditions that often work together to form metamorphic rock. Heat and pressure increase the deeper into Earth a rock is pushed. Temperature may cause metamorphic changes starting around 300°F (150°C).

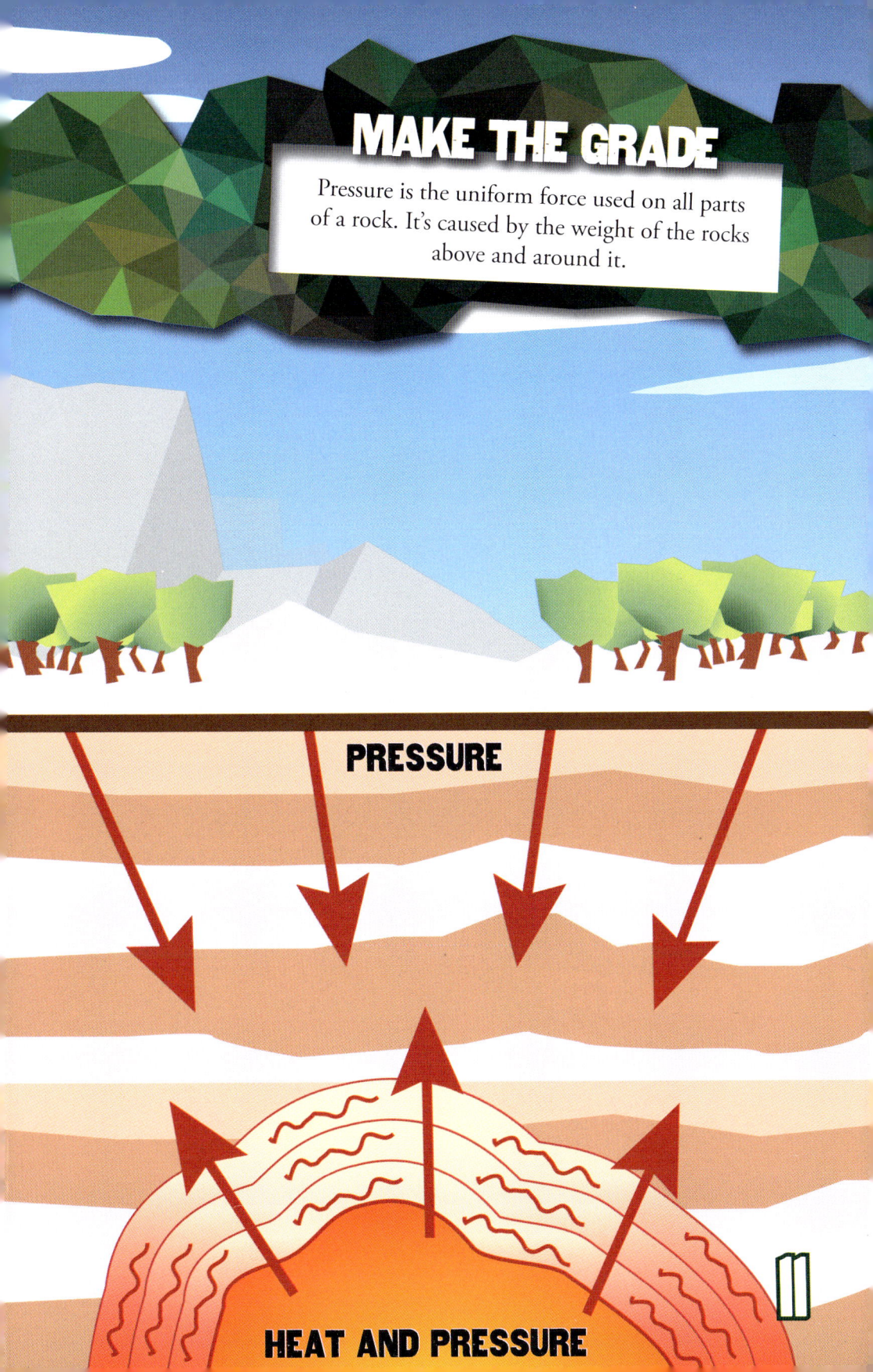

MAKE THE GRADE

Pressure is the uniform force used on all parts of a rock. It's caused by the weight of the rocks above and around it.

PRESSURE

HEAT AND PRESSURE

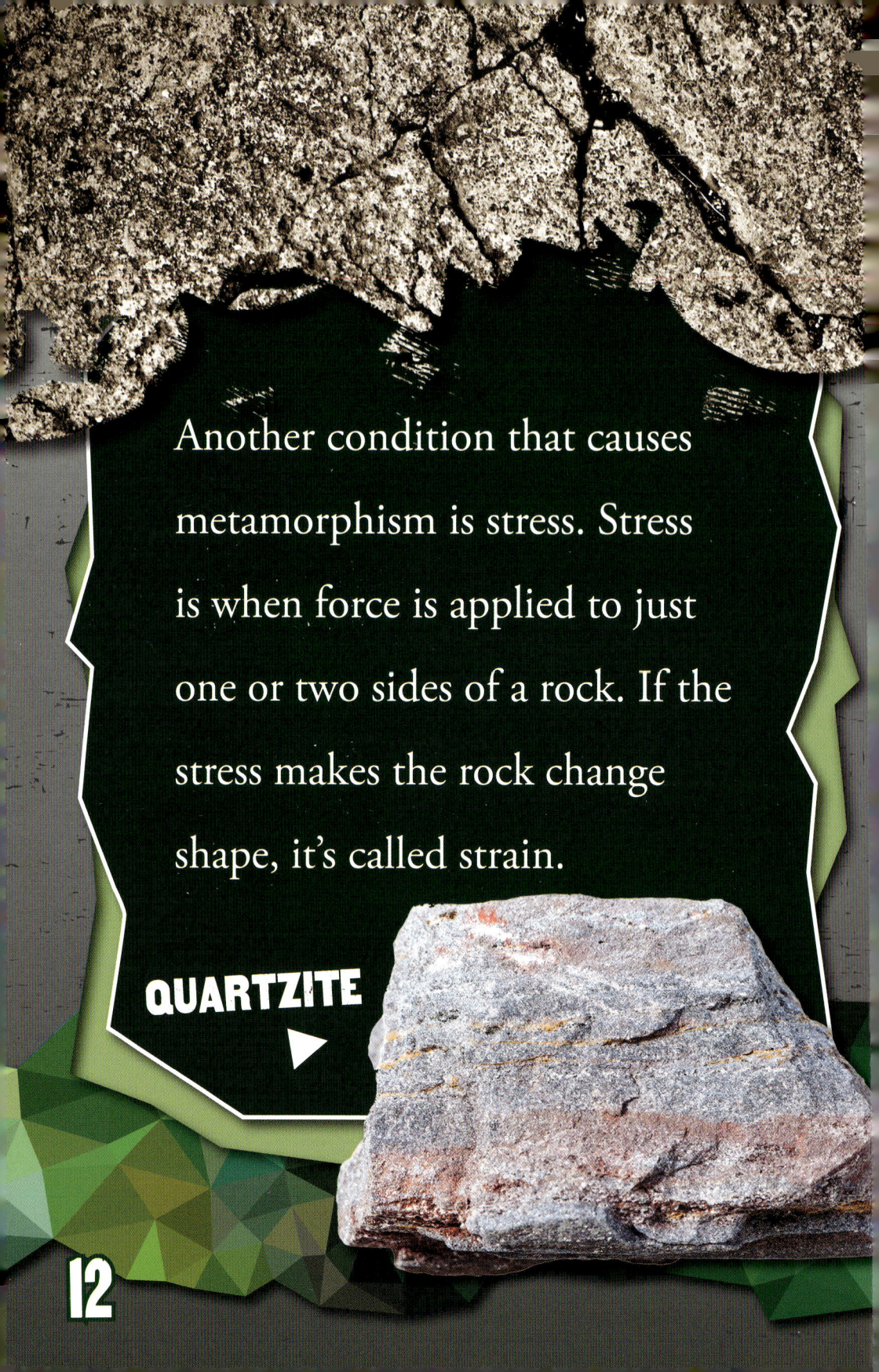

Another condition that causes metamorphism is stress. Stress is when force is applied to just one or two sides of a rock. If the stress makes the rock change shape, it's called strain.

QUARTZITE ▶

MAKE THE GRADE

Fluids, or liquids in a rock, can also put pressure on rock and play a part in forming metamorphic rock.

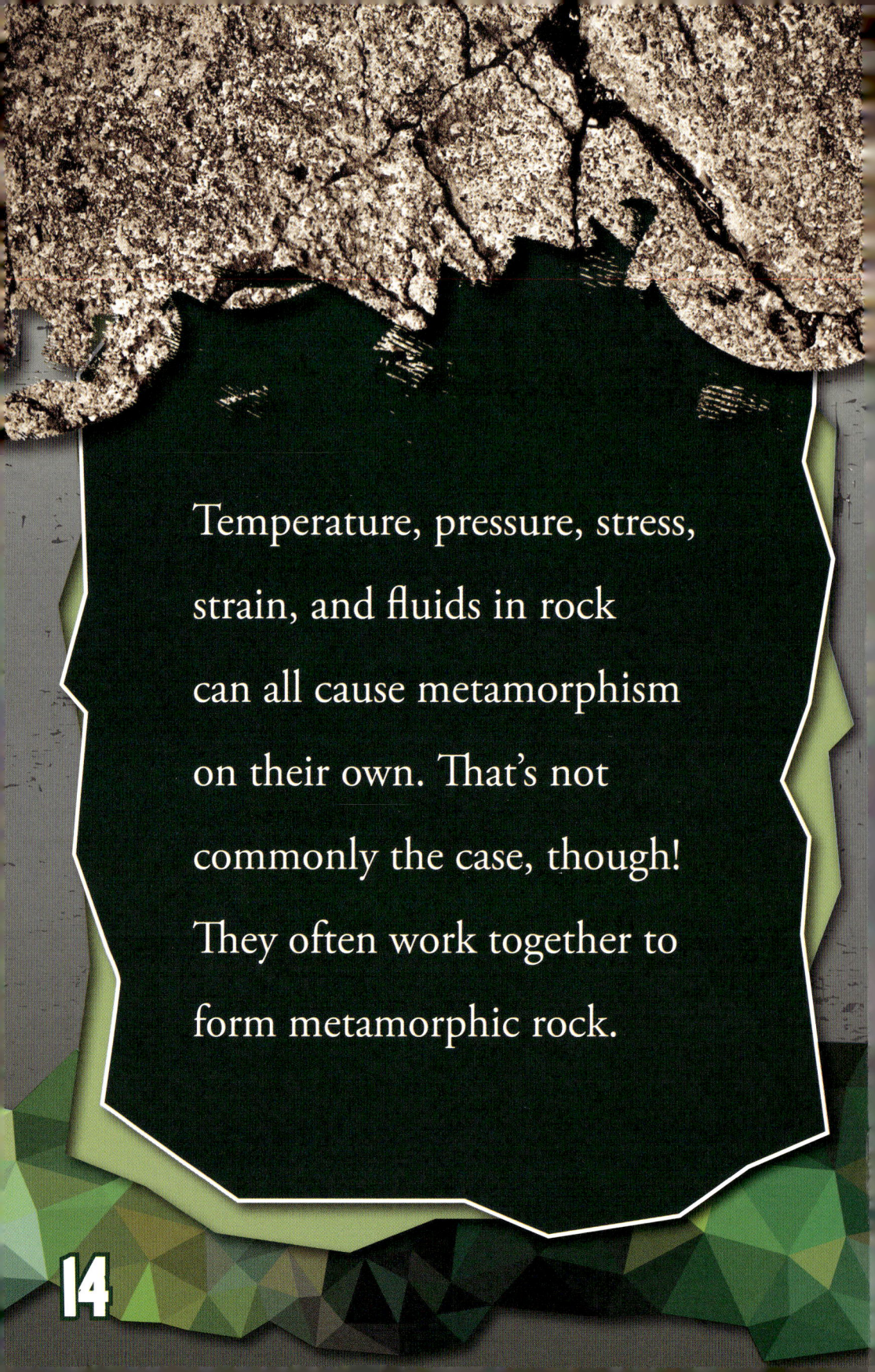

Temperature, pressure, stress, strain, and fluids in rock can all cause metamorphism on their own. That's not commonly the case, though! They often work together to form metamorphic rock.

GRANITE
IGNEOUS ROCK

▶

GNEISS
METAMORPHIC ROCK

MAKE THE GRADE

The physical and chemical changes metamorphic rocks have undergone make them **denser** than they were before.

WHERE'S THE ROCK?

Earth's surface, or crust, is made up of big pieces of rock called tectonic plates. Places where tectonic plates meet often have **earthquakes** and **volcanoes**. They also have a lot of metamorphic rock! Earthquakes and volcanoes cause big changes in the conditions around existing rock.

MAKE THE GRADE

Tectonic plates slide past one another, move over and under each other, and crash together.

KINDS OF METAMORPHISM

Regional metamorphism happens over a large area when tectonic plates or other bodies of rock move. They slide past each other or crash together, pushing rock deeper into Earth or lifting it up. Temperature and pressure commonly increase, and stress and strain may occur.

MOVEMENT OF TECTONIC PLATES

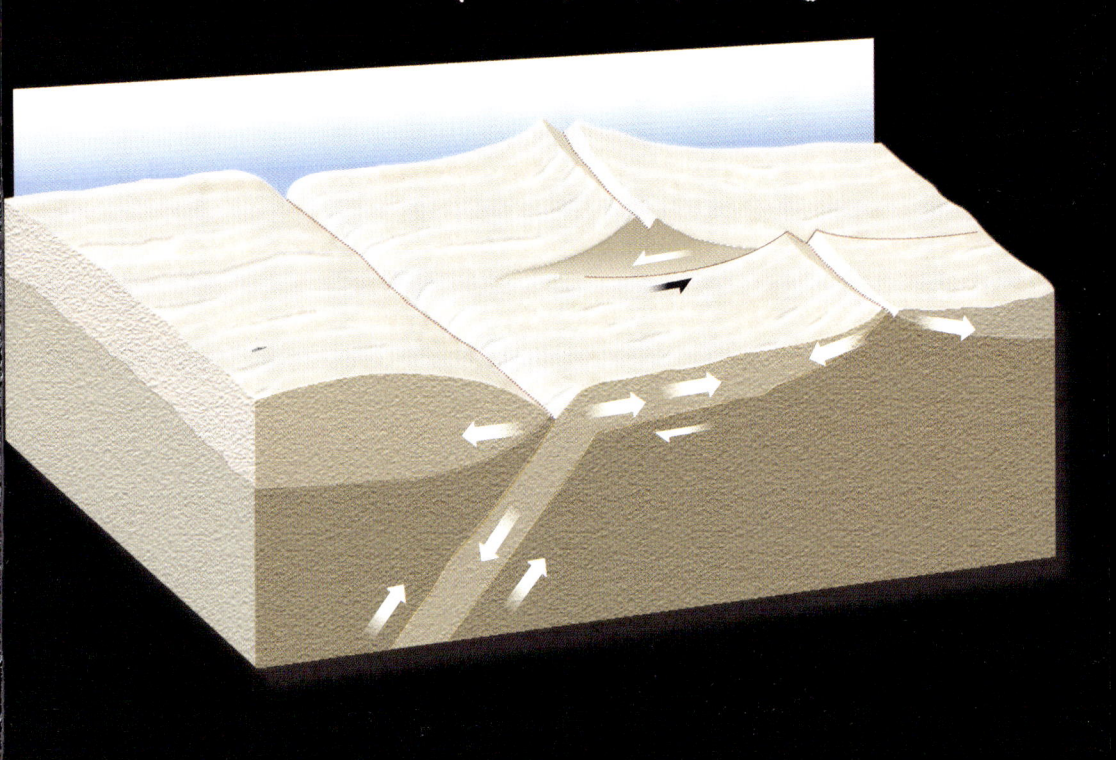

MAKE THE GRADE

Metamorphic rock that has formed by regional metamorphism is at the heart of many mountain ranges.

19

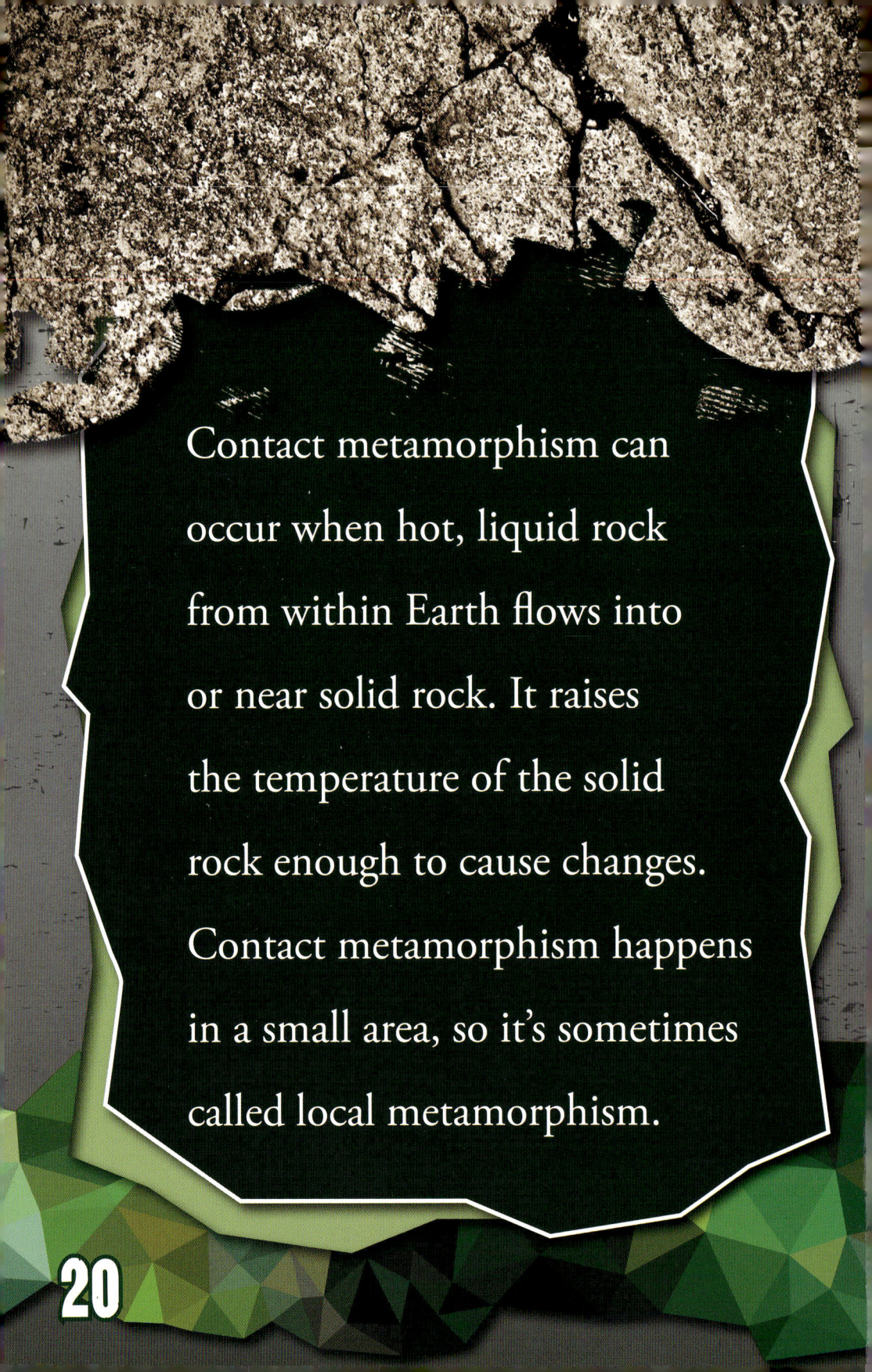

Contact metamorphism can occur when hot, liquid rock from within Earth flows into or near solid rock. It raises the temperature of the solid rock enough to cause changes. Contact metamorphism happens in a small area, so it's sometimes called local metamorphism.

MAKE THE GRADE

The hot, liquid rock inside Earth is called magma. When it reaches Earth's surface, it's called lava.

TEXTURE

Scientists commonly use a rock's texture to help **identify** it. Metamorphic rock can be found with two different textures, foliated and nonfoliated. Metamorphic rock with a foliated texture has many minerals you can see in layers or bands.

MAKE THE GRADE

When talking about rocks, "texture" means the size of a mineral's crystals or **grains** in a rock.

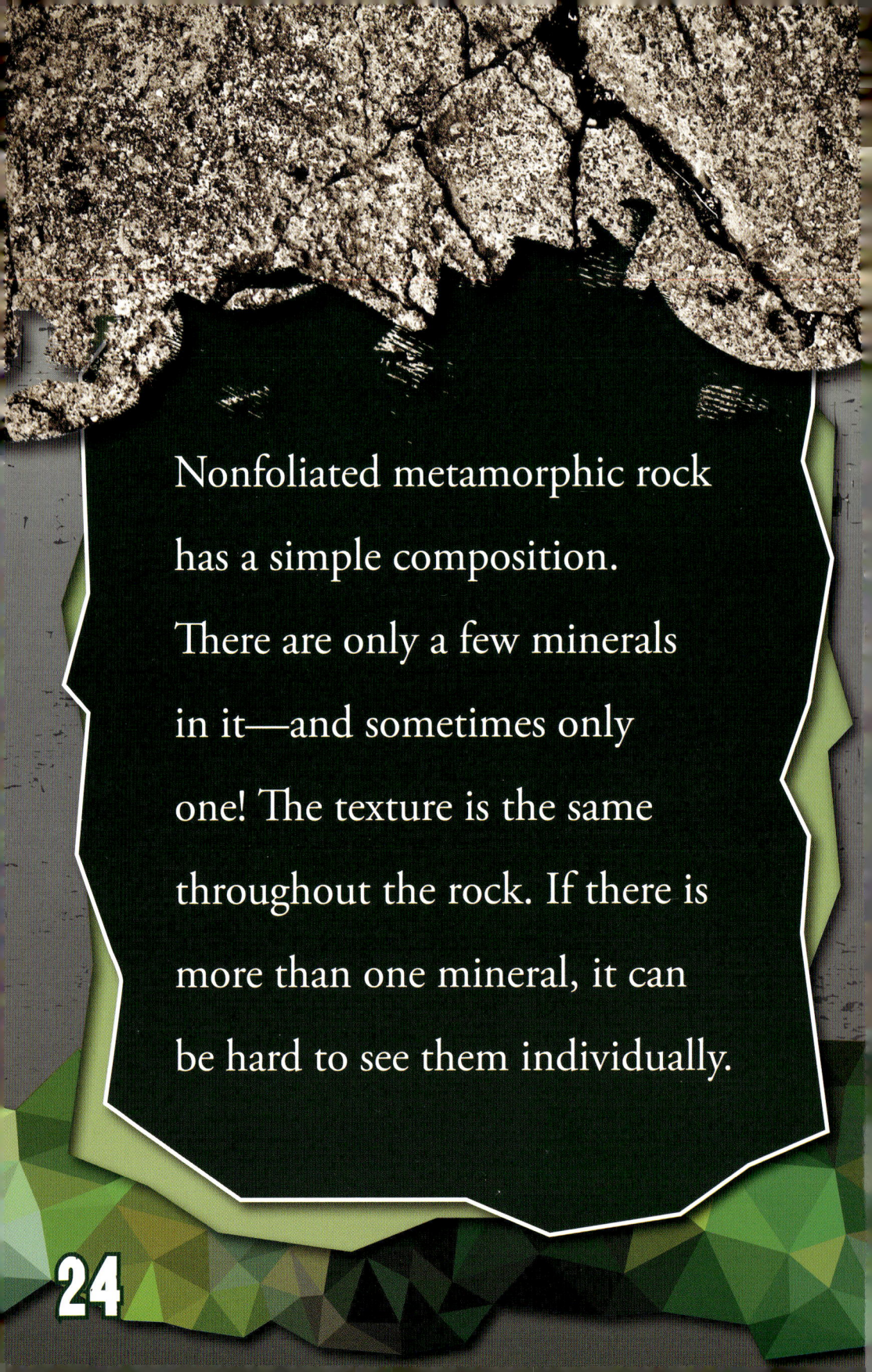

Nonfoliated metamorphic rock has a simple composition. There are only a few minerals in it—and sometimes only one! The texture is the same throughout the rock. If there is more than one mineral, it can be hard to see them individually.

MAKE THE GRADE

In addition to texture, scientists use color and hardness to identify rocks. They consider cleavage, or how a rock looks when it breaks, too.

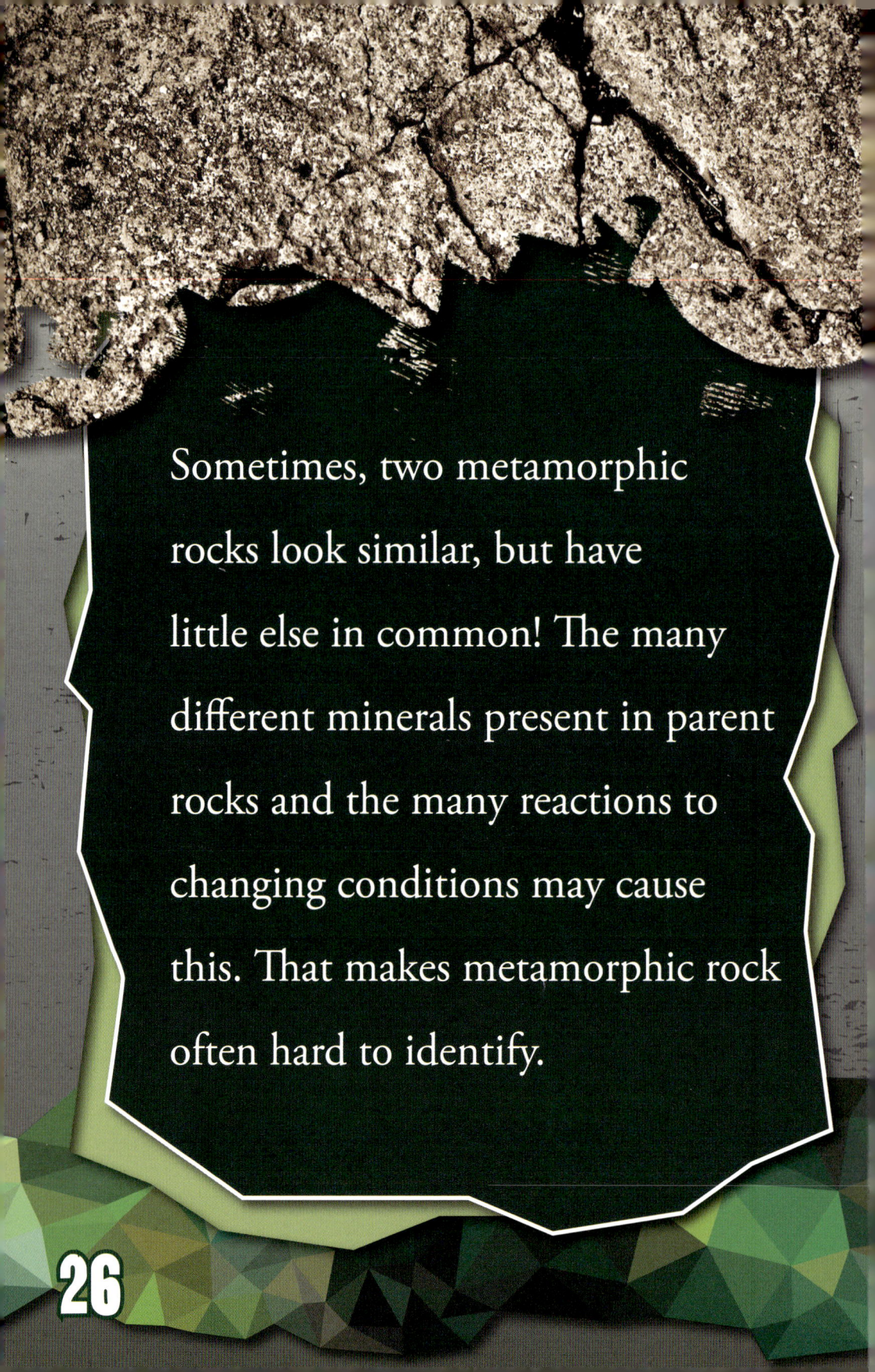

Sometimes, two metamorphic rocks look similar, but have little else in common! The many different minerals present in parent rocks and the many reactions to changing conditions may cause this. That makes metamorphic rock often hard to identify.

SLATE
METAMORPHIC ROCK

▷

PHYLLITE
METAMORPHIC ROCK

MAKE THE GRADE

"Parent rock" is the rock a metamorphic rock formed from.

SCHIST

Schist is one kind of metamorphic rock. It's any foliated metamorphic rock that features large, flat minerals in thin layers. Schist can form from any kind of rock and more than one kind of metamorphism!

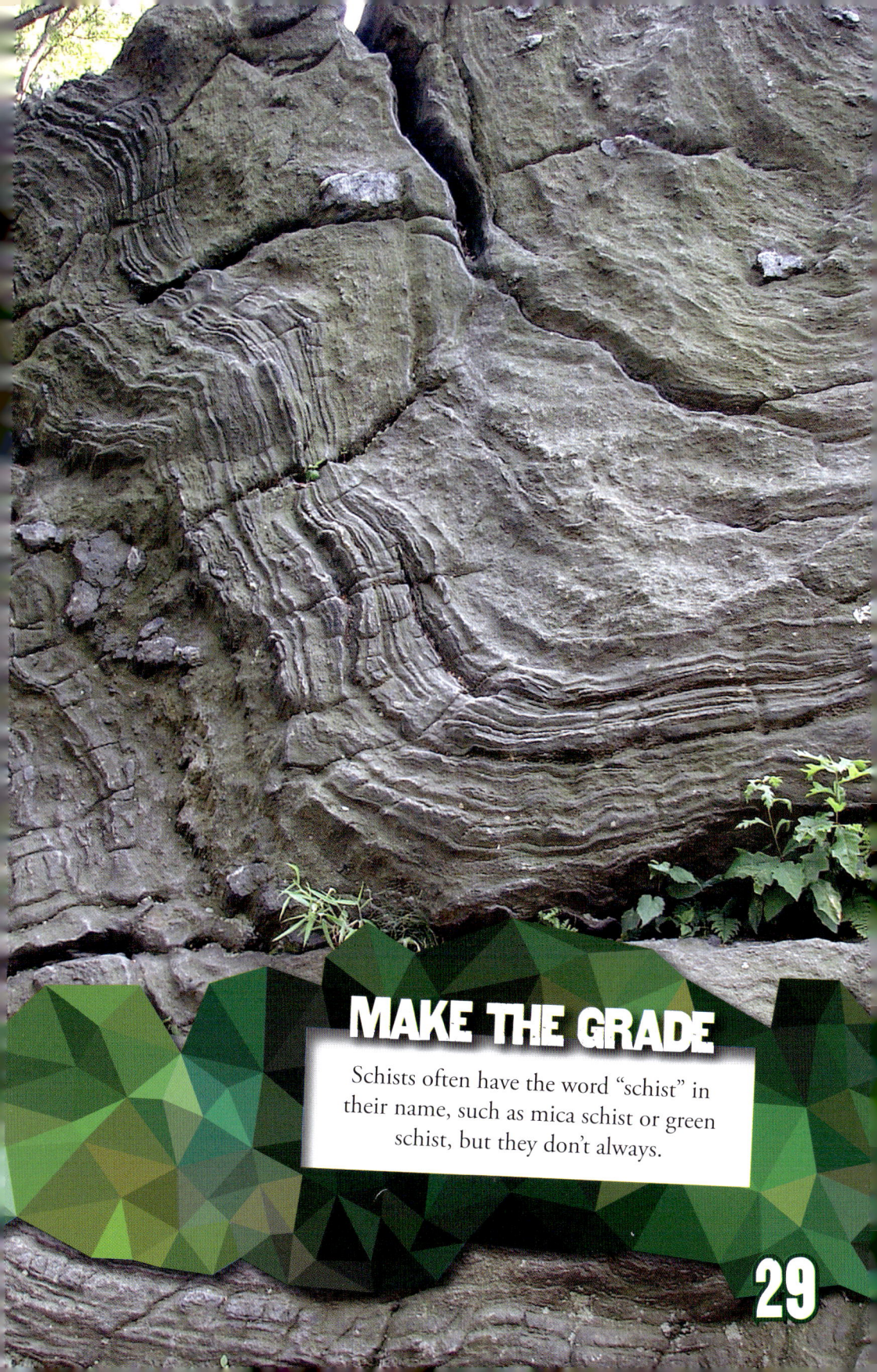

MAKE THE GRADE

Schists often have the word "schist" in their name, such as mica schist or green schist, but they don't always.

HOW DOES METAMORPHIC ROCK FORM?

EXISTING ROCK

↓ ↓

TECTONIC PLATES OR OTHER LARGE ROCK BODIES MEET

MAGMA FLOWS INTO OR NEAR ROCK

↓ ↓

CONDITIONS AROUND ROCK CHANGE, INCLUDING HEAT, PRESSURE, STRESS, OR STRAIN

MAGMA'S HIGH TEMPERATURE HEATS COOLER ROCK

↓ ↓

ROCK CHANGES (PHYSICALLY, CHEMICALLY, OR BOTH) TO STAY STABLE IN NEW CONDITIONS

GLOSSARY

chemical: matter that can be mixed with other matter to cause changes

dense: packed very closely together

earthquake: a shaking of the ground caused by the movement of Earth's crust

grain: a small, hard piece of mineral

identify: to find out the name or features of something

igneous: having to do with the rock that forms when hot, liquid rock from within Earth rises and cools

physical: having to do with the form of something

process: a series of steps or actions taken to complete something

react: to respond in a certain way

sedimentary: having to do with the rock that forms when sand, stones, and other matter are pressed together over a long time

stable: not likely to change suddenly or greatly

volcano: an opening in Earth's surface through which hot, liquid rock sometimes flows

FOR MORE INFORMATION

BOOKS

Brannon, Cecelia H. *A Look at Metamorphic Rocks*. New York, NY: Enslow Publishing, 2016.

Dee, Willa. *Earth's Rock Cycle*. New York, NY: PowerKids Press, 2014.

WEBSITES

Metamorphic Rock
scienceforkidsclub.com/metamorphic-rock.html
Review how metamorphic rocks form here.

The Rock Cycle
eschooltoday.com/rocks/the-rock-cycle.html
Use this interactive website to learn more about the rock cycle.

Publisher's note to educators and parents: Our editors have carefully reviewed these websites to ensure that they are suitable for students. Many websites change frequently, however, and we cannot guarantee that a site's future contents will continue to meet our high standards of quality and educational value. Be advised that students should be closely supervised whenever they access the Internet.

INDEX

contact metamorphism 20
fluids 13, 14
heat 10, 30
magma 21, 30
minerals 7, 8, 9, 22, 23, 24, 26, 28
parent rock 26, 27
pressure 10, 11, 13, 14, 18, 30
regional metamorphism 18, 19
strain 12, 14, 18, 30
stress 12, 14, 18, 30
tectonic plates 16, 17, 18, 30
temperature 10, 14, 18, 20, 30
texture 22, 23, 24, 25